Text written and compiled by Su Box
Illustrations copyright © 1994, 1995 Carolyn Cox
This edition copyright © 2003 Lion Publishing

The moral rights of the author and illustrator
have been asserted

Published by
Lion Publishing plc
Mayfield House, 256 Banbury Road,
Oxford OX2 7DH, England
www.lion-publishing.co.uk
ISBN 0 7459 4815 4

First edition 2003
10 9 8 7 6 5 4 3 2 1 0

A catalogue record for this book is available
from the British Library

Typeset in 13/18 Baskerville MT Schoolbook
Printed and bound in Singapore

My Book of Prayers

Written and compiled by Su Box
Illustrated by Carolyn Cox

LION
Children's Books

Contents

My World

My Day

Our World

Sad Days

Happy Days

Introduction

Do you ever talk to God, or pray? Many people pray in church or at bedtime, but did you know that you can pray at any time and in any place? God wants us to talk to him about everything and he understands how we are feeling. Sometimes we are not sure what to say, so the prayers in this book may help. You will find prayers to say on ordinary days and on special days through the year.

If you like, you can change the words a little or add the name of the person or event you are praying for, to make a prayer just right for you to say. You will soon have some favourite prayers in this book, and others may give you ideas about what you might like to say to God.

Prayer is
Talking to God,
Listening to God,
Loving God.

Alison Winn

My World

Hello God

Here I am
beneath the sky
and all alone
in prayer;
but I know
God is listening,
for God is
everywhere.

Lois Rock

My head is still.
My hands are still.
My arms are still.
My feet are still.
And now I fold my hands to pray.

Author unknown

When you can't put your prayers
into words, God hears your heart.

Author unknown

Thank you, God, that you care for me
and all I do each day.
Thank you that I can pray to you
for you hear what I say.
You are there when I'm glad or sad,
and even when I'm wrong.
I praise you, God, for loving me
right now and all life long.

All About Me

Lord, you know all about me…
I praise you because you made me
In an amazing and wonderful way.
Based on Psalm 139

Thank you, God, for making me,
All that I am, and all that I can see.
Thank you too for your loving care
For all your creation everywhere.

Dear God,
Here I am: your child, full of life and
eager to learn about your world.

You made me just as I am, God.
Thank you that there's no one quite
like me anywhere else in the world.
That makes me feel really special.

My Family: the Grown-ups

Dear God,
Thank you for Mum and Dad who give me
so much, especially lots of love. Help me to
show them that I love them too.

Help me, God, to listen to my parents
and to hear the wise words they say.

Dear God,
Thank you for my mum and dad;
They've lots to do today.
Help them finish really soon
So we'll have time to play.

Dear God, it can't be easy to grow old.
Give me patience when Granny and Grandad
forget things. Help me to listen when they
want to talk. One day I'll be old too.

My Family:
Brothers and Sisters

Dear God,
It's not always easy to have brothers or sisters.
But sometimes it's really great. Please help us
to get along together.

> Dear God,
> Sometimes I wish I had a brother or
> sister to play with. Please help me not
> to feel lonely.

We're so happy to have a new baby
in our family. Thank you, God!

Dear God, thank you for my sister.
She always understands how I feel.

Olwen Turchetta

My Family: All Together

God bless all those that I love;
God bless all those that love me;
God bless all those that love those that I love
And all those that love those that love me.

From a New England sampler

Thank you for the love we show
when we hug each other.

Dear God,
I'm glad that your son, Jesus, lived
in a family. He knows the fun and the
difficult things about living with others.
Help our family to be happy, safe
and loving.

Our Home

Mum says that our home is more than a house
because it is furnished with love. Thank you,
God, for my family and for your love.

Dear God, I pray for children
who live in unhappy homes.
Please help them not to be sad.

May our home be happy
May our home be safe
May our home be loving
May our home be blessed.

Lois Rock

Bless this house which is our home
May we welcome all who come.

Anonymous

Loving Father, hear my prayer,
For all your creatures everywhere;
For animals both big and small,
And for my pets – please bless them all.

Mary Batchelor

My Day

In the Morning

This morning, God,
This is your day.
I am your child,
Show me your way.
Amen

Author unknown

This is the day the Lord has made;
let us rejoice and be glad in it.

Psalm 118:24

Father, we thank you for the night,
And for the pleasant morning light;
For rest and food and loving care,
And all that makes the day so fair.
Help us to do the things we should,
To be to others kind and good;
In all we do at work or play
To grow more loving every day.

Author unknown

Dear God,
Thank you for this new day.
Amen

At Mealtimes

God is great, God is good,
Let us thank him for our food.

Traditional

Each time we eat,
May we remember God's love.

A Chinese grace

For what we are about to receive
May the Lord make us truly thankful.

Traditional

Bless, dear Lord, my daily food.
Make me strong and make me good.

A.C. Osborn Hann

The bread is warm and fresh,
The water cool and clear.
Lord of all life, be with us,
Lord of all life, be near.

An African grace

For good food and good friends to share it,
thank you, God.

At School

Lord Jesus Christ, be with me today,
And help me in all I think, or do, or say.

Traditional

Bless to me, O Lord,
the work of my hands.
Bless to me, O God,
the work of my mind.
Bless to me, O God,
the work of my heart.

Author unknown

Dear God,
When I don't know the right answer,
please help me ask the right question.

Lois Rock

Dear God, every day I learn something new.
Thank you that the world is
so full of amazing things.

Sarah Medina

29

At Play

For all the strength I have
To run and jump and play,
For making me just as I am
I thank you, God, today.

Mary Batchelor (adapted)

Computer games and model trains and skates and bikes and kites. We thank you, God, for all the different ways we can enjoy playing together.

Dear God, help me to be a good loser.

Jesus, may I be like you;
Loving, kind in all I do;
Kind and happy when I play
Close beside you all the day.
M. Ensor

Dear God,
Thank you for sunny days when I can play outside with my friends and for rainy days when I can enjoy reading my books.
Olwen Turchetta

My Friends

Thank you for the happy times
I shared with my friends today.
Thank you for the memories
We'll enjoy another day.

> Dear God,
> Thank you for my friend next door,
> And my friend across the street,
> And please help me to be a friend
> To each and every one I meet.
> Amen
> *Anonymous*

Thank you, God, that none of us is quite the same. I like having friends who enjoy playing and sharing different things with me.

Thank you, God, for all my friends. Help me to be a good friend and not to argue or let them down. Thank you, most of all, for being my best friend.

For lonely children everywhere
Who do not have someone to care.
Dear God, I pray that you will send
A loving, kind and special friend.

Author unknown

Dear God,
Help me not to tread thoughtlessly
on the feelings of my friends.

Dear God,
Forgive me for saying hurtful things to my friend.
Give me the courage to say that I'm sorry, and
help me to be gentle with my words.

Dear God,
Help me to be friendly to those who have
no friends.

Dear God,
When others are sad, help me to comfort them,
just as my friends comfort me.

At Night

Dear God, sometimes I get scared in the dark.
Help me to remember that you are right here
with me, so I am never really alone.

Now I lay me down to sleep,
I pray thee, Lord, thy child to keep;
Thy love to guard me through the night
And wake me in the morning light.

Traditional

Now the day is over,
Night is drawing nigh,
Shadows of the evening
Steal across the sky.

Through the long night-watches
May thine angels spread
Their white wings above me,
Watching round my bed.

Sabine Baring-Gould

Lord, keep us safe this night,
Secure from all our fears;
May angels guard us while we sleep,
Till morning light appears.

John Leland

Day is done,
Gone the sun
From the lake,
From the hills,
From the sky.
Safely rest,
All is well!
God is nigh.

Anonymous

When I lie down, I go to sleep in peace;
you alone, O Lord, keep me perfectly safe.

Psalm 4:8

Our World

The World Around Us

All things bright and beautiful,
All creatures great and small,
All things wise and wonderful,
The Lord God made them all.

Mrs C.F. Alexander

Lord God Almighty,
how great and wonderful
are your deeds!

Revelation 15:3

Dear God,
Thank you for making this
wonderful world. There's so
much to see and so many
things to enjoy.

God made the world so broad and grand
Filled with blessing from his hand.
He made the sky so high and blue,
And all the little children, too.

Anonymous

Creator God, we praise you for our world:
for the high snowy mountains and fertile
green valleys, the leafy jungles and sandy
deserts, and rivers that flow into the sea.
Thank you for making so many wonderful,
different places.

Dear God,
May we learn to see the world as you see it.
May we learn to care for the world as you do.

O God, the more I explore your world,
the more I marvel at it.

God, who made the earth,
The air, the sky, the sea,
Who gave the light its birth,
Careth for me.

God, who made the grass,
The flower, the fruit, the tree,
The day and night to pass,
Careth for me.

God, who made all things,
On earth, in air, in sea,
Who changing seasons brings,
Careth for me.

Sarah Betts Rhodes

People of the World

From all that dwells below the skies,
Let faith and hope with joy arise;
Let beauty, truth and good be sung
Through every land, by every tongue.

A Unitarian prayer

This I know in heaven above,
All hope and joy are there.
In the circle of God's love,
There's room for all –
And to spare.

A spiritual

Dear Lord, Creator of the world,
Help us to love one another,
Help us care for one another
As sister or as brother.
May friendship grow
From nation to nation.
Bring peace to our world
Dear Lord of Creation.

Anonymous

All God's Creatures

O God, help me to be kind
to all living things.

Dear God,
Thank you for making so many different animals. Help us to learn to treat them well so that we may all enjoy sharing your world.

Dear God,
Help me to remember that even scary animals and insects and snakes are part of your creation and should be treated with respect.

He prayeth best, who loveth best
All things both great and small;
For the dear God who loveth us,
He made and loveth all.

Samuel Taylor Coleridge

Thank you for the beasts so tall,
Thank you for the creatures small.
Thank you for all things that live,
Thank you, God, for all you give.

H.W. Dobson

Dear Father, hear and bless
Thy beasts and singing birds,
And guard with tenderness
Small things that have no words.

Margaret Wise Brown

Praise God for the animals
for the colours of them,
for the spots and stripes of them,
for the patches and plains of them,
their claws and paws.

Lynn Warren

Animals great, animals small,
Thank you, God, that you care for them all.

In Town

God of all our cities,
Each alley, street and square,
Please look down on every house
And bless the people there.

Joan Gale Thomas

Busy shops and crowded places,
Hectic day and night.
Noisy streets and unknown faces,
Bustle, sounds and light.
All exciting, sometimes frightening,
Town life can be hard,
But you're with us, caring for us
Thank you, Father God.

Please make this town safe
for young and old,
for rich and poor,
and for people of all races
and places.

In the Country

Dear God,
Thank you for making the beautiful countryside.
Help us not to spoil it for other people or for the
animals that live there.

Thank you for wide, open places, where
we can run and play in the fresh air and
listen to the sounds of the country.

For flowers that bloom about our feet,
Father, we thank Thee,
For tender grass so fresh and sweet,
Father, we thank Thee,
For the song of bird and hum of bee,
For all things fair we hear or see,
Father in heaven, we thank Thee.

Ralph Waldo Emerson

I thank you, God,
for the high skies
that stretch up
to heaven.

The Weather

Dear Lord on high
Make a clear sky
Make the day fine
And let the sweet sun shine.

Traditional

Dear God, thank you for the rain which cleans
our world and gives us water.

The sun may shine
The snow may fall
God will always
Love us all.

Victoria Tebbs

If I had my way I'd pray
to have fine weather every day.
But farmers need refreshing rain
and then warm sun to ripen grain.
So, dear God, I pray tonight
you'll send the weather you think right.

The Seasons

Thank you, Creator God, for the unchanging
pattern of the seasons that tells of your
never-ending love for your world.

Thank you, God, that we can use
our senses to enjoy:
… seeing the bright spring colours
… smelling the scent of summer flowers
… tasting the juicy autumn fruits
… touching the soft winter snow
and hearing birdsong all year long.

Thank you, God, for sunshine,
Thank you, God, for spring.
Thank you, God, for sending
Every lovely thing.

Mary Batchelor

Caring for the World

Dear God,

I'm sorry we have spoiled your world. Please help us to look after it better. Help us to care for the land and all that grows on it and to save all the animals in danger.

Generous God,
I know you give me all I need –
To ask for more is sometimes greed.
But many people are quite poor;
I ask that you will give them more.
Amen

People don't always care.
They make wild creatures rare,
cutting down all the trees,
polluting lakes and seas.
We're sorry for this mess –
it must cause you distress.
We need to change things now,
so please, God, show us how.

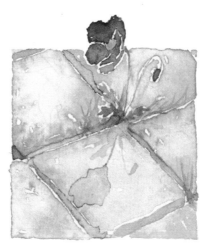

Dear God,
You planted the Garden of Eden.
May we treat the wild lands as sacred.
You built the Heavenly City.
May we know that we build our cities
on holy ground.

Lois Rock

Sad Days

Illness

Dear God, when I am in pain please comfort me.

Thank you, God, for doctors, nurses and the many other people who help sick people to get better. Please bless their work of healing.

Dear God,
I feel poorly today. Please help me to get well soon and to be patient until I feel better.

Loving God,
Be close to those who are ill;
Comfort those who are worried;
Help those who are in pain.
May they know your love and care.

Help me, kind God, to show your love and kindness to my friends and family when they are ill.

The Hardest Goodbye

Every day
in silence we remember
those whom we loved
to whom we have said a last goodbye.
Every day
in silence we remember.

Lois Rock

Dear God,
You know how it feels
when someone you
love dies. Please be
close to me now as
I feel so sad.
Amen

I didn't like saying
my last goodbye
today, God. Then
I remembered that
those you love have
a new home in
heaven.

Difficult Days

Dear God,
I have a difficult decision to make today.
Help me to do the right thing.

> Dear God,
> It's hard when people don't understand me.
> Thank you that you know me better than
> anyone else.

Jesus, you know what it is like to stand up for
what is right. Sometimes you had to face people
who were unfriendly and unkind. Help me when
I have to do the same.

> Dear God,
> Help me to see my faults more clearly
> than the wrongdoings of other people.

Dear God,
Knowing you are with me when I'm sad is
like knowing that the sun is only hidden behind
the clouds.

Sometimes we're mean and selfish, God,
And spoil somebody's day.
You are loving and fair to all;
Help us to live your way.

Someone hurt my feelings today.
Now I feel bad about them and
it won't be easy to forgive them.
Please help me to treat that person
the way I want to be treated.

Dear God,
I am sorry for what I've done wrong
and I ask that you will forgive me.

When Things Go Wrong

Dear God,
Bring peace to the whole world.

There are many bad things happening
in the world. People are fighting, some
have nowhere to live and many don't have
enough food to eat. Please show us how
we can help, God.

Lord, I know you love what is fair
and hate it when people put others down
and do all kinds of wrong things. Please
help more people to think as you do.

Based on Amos 2:6–7

Dear God, please help people who are being
treated unfairly or facing danger not to be afraid.
Amen

Please Help, God

Lord God,
Help me to become the person
you want me to be.

> Please bring:
> Peace in my heart;
> Peace in my home;
> Peace in my street;
> Peace in my world.
>
> *Lois Rock*

Father God, help me to enjoy the things
I have and not to always want more.

O God, I don't understand why bad things
happen to good people; but I want to learn to
do good things even to bad people.

Lois Rock

Dear God, when I'm scared please help me to remember that you are stronger than anything that frightens me.

Happy Days

Holidays

Thank you, God,
For special days to look forward to,
and special days to remember.

Felicity Henderson

For days at home and far away
I thank you God today.
For friends and family come to stay
I thank you God today.
For Mum and Dad and time to play
I thank you God today.
For all the fun of our holiday
I thank you God today.

Thank you, God, for this summer day,
Thank you, God, for this golden day,
Thank you, God, for this lazy day,
Thank you, God, for our holiday.

Lois Rock

Birthdays

Guide me in my growing older,
Wiser, gentler,
Braver, bolder.

Lois Rock

Dear God,
Thank you for my birthday
And all I've done this year.
Some things were good,
Some times were sad,
But you were always near.

Thank you, God, for my birthday. The party
was fun, the presents were great and everyone
made me feel really special. Help me
to remember to give and share,
so that I can make other people's
birthdays special too.

Father God, please be with me in all
that happens in this new year.

Sundays

Thank you, God, for all you have done for us.
Let people everywhere praise you!

Based on Psalm 67:7

Thank you, kind God, for your day of rest.
May we spend its hours on things that bring
us joy.

Lois Rock

After you had made the world
You had a day of rest
When we get too busy, Lord,
Remind us your plan's best.

May I feel you very near
When I stop to pray.
Help me listen when you send
A message for today.

At Christmas

Thank you, God, for all the presents we receive at Christmas. Help me to remember that all happiness comes from you.

Dear God, please give your love to anyone who has no one to love them at Christmas.

Thank you, God, for showing your love by giving us the best present ever – your son, Jesus. Help us to share Christmas love with everyone we meet.

Thank you for sending Jesus to be the light of the world and to show your light.

At Easter

Lord Jesus, you suffered pain and hurt for us;
You died on the cross to take away our sin.
Thank you for loving us so much.
Help us to love you too.

Mary Batchelor

Dear Jesus, it hurt you on the cross. But you got better, and you made EVERYTHING better again.

A child's prayer

Good Friday is a time of sadness,
Easter is a time of gladness.
On Good Friday Jesus died
But rose again at Eastertide.
All thanks and praise to God.

Mary Batchelor

Friday sunset, black and red.
Weep, for Jesus Christ is dead.
Sunday sunrise, white and gold.
Christ is risen, as foretold.

Lois Rock

Jesus Christ is risen today.
Alleluia!

Based on Surrexit Christus hodie

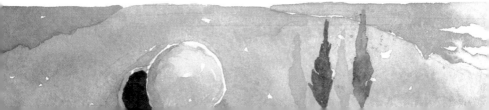

Harvest

Dear God in paradise
Look upon our sowing:
Bless the little gardens
And the green things growing.

Anonymous

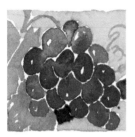

O God, you show your care for the land by sending rain; you make it rich and fertile. What a rich harvest your goodness provides!

Psalm 65:9, 11

Thank you, God, for giving us a good harvest. All that you give us you mean us to share. Help us to share these gifts with others so that the world may be a better place.

The sun and the rain,
The seeds that bring grain,
The fruit and the flowers,
That grow with the showers.
Thank you, God, for all
your harvest gifts.

Thank You, God

Dear God, thank you that each one of us is special to you and that you love and care for us always.

Thank you for the world so sweet,
Thank you for the food we eat,
Thank you for the birds that sing,
Thank you, God, for everything.

Edith Rutter Leatham

Thank you, Lord, for dying for us. Thank you
for loving us even though we do things wrong
and sometimes forget you.

Lord, it is good to give you thanks
from morning to night.

Based on Psalm 92:1–2

Glory to God for everything!

St John Chrysostom

You're Great, God!

Sing praise to the Lord!
Sing praise!

Based on Psalm 47:6

I praise you, God, for your great love for each one
of us. Help me to light up my world with your love.

> Dear God,
> I just feel good knowing that you
> are everywhere. That's all.
>
> *A child's prayer from Sweden*

Please fill my life, O Lord my God,
In every part with praise,
That every day I'll show to all
Your being and your ways.

After Horatius Bonar

Our Father God,
We want you to be our King for ever:
then everyone will live as you want.
Give us each day all that we need.
Forgive us for the wrong things we do,
as we forgive people who hurt us.
Help us stop wanting to do bad things.
And keep us from all harm.
Amen

Adapted from the prayer Jesus taught,
the Lord's Prayer

First Line Index

Acknowledgments

Thanks go to all those who have given permission to include material in this book, as indicated in the list below. Every effort has been made to trace and contact copyright owners. We apologize for any inadvertent omissions or errors.

All unattributed prayers are by Su Box, copyright © 2003 Lion Publishing. Prayers by Felicity Henderson (p. 76), Sarah Medina (p. 29), Lois Rock (pp.10, 20, 29, 60, 64, 72, 77, 78, 81 & 85), Victoria Tebbs (p. 55) and Olwen Turchetta (pp.16 & 31) are copyright © Lion Publishing. Prayer by Alison Winn (p.8) used by permission of Candle Books. Prayers by Mary Batchelor (pp. 22, 30, 57, 84, 85) are copyright © Mary Batchelor. Prayer by A.C. Osborn Hann (p.27) from *Baby's First Prayers* and prayers by M. Ensor (p. 31) and Edith Rutter Leatham (p. 89) from *Hymns and Songs for Children* are used by permission of SPCK. Prayer by H.W. Dobson (p. 48) from *In Excelsis* is used by permission of the National Society for Promoting Religious Education. Prayer (p.48) copyright © 1943, 1950 by Margaret Wise Brown. Copyright renewed 1978 by Roberta B. Rauch. Used by permission of HarperCollins Publishers. Prayer by Joan Gale Thomas (p. 50) used by permission of Deborah Sheppard. A child's prayer (p. 84) is by Evie Money. Used by permission. A child's prayer from Sweden (p. 90) from *Children in Conversation with God*, published by Anza A. Lema, copyright © Lutheran World Federation. Scripture quotation (p. 25) taken from the Holy Bible, New International Version, copyright © 1973, 1978, 1984 by International Bible Society. Used by permission of Hodder & Stoughton Limited. All rights reserved. 'NIV' is a registered trademark of International Bible Society. UK trademark number 1448790. Scriptures (pp. 38, 40, 87) quoted from the Good News Bible published by The Bible Societies/HarperCollins Publishers Ltd, UK © American Bible Society 1966, 1971, 1976, 1992, used with permission.